AF413318

From Profiles to Partners

A Successful Guide to Real Love

How to Attract, Recognize, and Fall in Love with Your Soulmate

Edward J. Jones

From Profiles to Partners:
A Successful Guide to Real Love
How to Attract, Recognize, and Fall in Love with Your Soulmate

ISBN 979-8-9916504-0-3

Dedication

This book is for my mother, Helen C. Jones, who inspired all her children to read, work hard, and think for themselves.

This book is also for the following people:

Mr. Oshima and my Shotokan Karate of America Seniors, who taught me how to "Face myself."

David Goddard, one of my spiritual Fathers, who guides me through the Mystical world of the Qabala.

The Drepung Loseling Institute for deepening my *understanding of the spiritual science of the mind and Karma*.

The Agape International Spiritual Center and Michael Beckwith's *The Answer Is You* for providing me with hope during my "dark night of the soul."

Diane Stein introduced me to the *Ageless Wisdom of Energy Healing*.

All men and women who live high functional morals and ethical standards. I pray each day for the personal and dating lives of those who have not given up hope.

All the players who have made dating challenging with lies, duplicity, dishonesty, pridefulness, promiscuity, and gaslighting. Thanks for all the lessons as I triumphantly rise above your games with my scars from a well-fought battle!

The Source of all divine inspiration: God the Father, God's Son, and the Holy Sprint whom I serve.

Acknowledgments

Thanks to my editor, Judy Carney, for her insights and guidance.

Thanks to Aylainah Garibay for proofreading my book and providing valuable spiritual insights.

I want to acknowledge the book cover design team, John and Lyndsey Lewellen.

About the Author

Edward is a Spiritual seeker who has been asking the Magical question "*Why?*" about the mysteries of Life's challenges.

My keys to self-discovery began when I studied Shotokan Karate and learned how to meditate to prepare for practice and to have stillness as we faced our weaknesses while pushing ourselves to the next level during intense, demanding practices. Next, I also discovered Reiki energy healing.

My first major spiritual initiation was through the book "*Mahatma I & II: The I Am Presence*" by Brian Grattan. This energy works with the Angelic realms to anchor the Divine Feminine and integrate the Divine

Masculine to bring us back to wholeness. I was also initiated as a "Living Triple Flame of Source" healer, a grand healing dispensation. This allows for the clearing and healing of karmic patterns and the activation of our true divine nature.

The next step in my journey came as I sought to understand my personal Karma and why my life was not working. I seemed stuck in a karmic loop and needed to figure out how Karma works. I studied Tibetan Buddhism at the Drepung Loseling Institute in Atlanta for several years. The Buddhists have a highly refined "Science of the Mind" and an understanding of how good and bad Karma are generated and can be cured. I also began Reiki energy healing. I am studying the Ageless Wisdom of the Qabalah with one of my spiritual fathers, David Goddard.

As my spiritual development and studies continued, I added Awakening Dynamics Theta Energy Healing to my portfolio. This technique allows for discovering subconscious energy blocks that may impede our alignment with our authentic selves. As these blocks are removed, it creates a space for downloading life-affirming programs. I also studied at the Agape International Spiritual Center. Some of their practitioner courses helped me develop a deeper understanding of Affirmative Prayer.

I have learned there are many ways to be a channel for the divine life of the "One Life" to express healing through us.

Contact me at www.fromprofilestopartners.love

Contents

Why Am I Writing This Book?

Ever since I was a small child, I dreamed of being a king married to my queen. At this young age, these are nothing but fairy tales that we are programmed with by the media. However, I did enjoy them! Let's see how these fantasies played out in my adult life. I have gone through three divorces and have been divorced since 2010. What happened to the fairy tale? How did my life become such a good example of a bad example of how not to choose a mate?

Hindsight is a perfect science as I contemplated each relationship. I learned to stop blaming them for their games. It was my choice to engage with them in the first place and continue the relationship while my intuition was screaming at me because I was allowing myself to be exploited. I still hold fast to the dream of finding my soulmate. I have met some incredible women; however, they are in relationships, or we are not right for each other.

As I continued my spiritual journey and my personal development, I slowly realized that I was the source of all the drama based on my immaturity and unconscious choices, attitudes, and behaviors. As I began "waking up," I incorporated daily spiritual studies and practices, including meditation, forgiveness, energy healing, and visioning. I realize I must live up to the high-minded virtues I desire to be ready for my soulmate, who will have similar consciousness and values.

Some may ask why I continue to pursue a deep spiritual, mental, emotional, physical, loving, romantic, sensual, empowering, and compassionate relationship when we have a 50% divorce rate for first-time marriages. It is higher for second and third marriages. **Chapter 2, Relationship Karma,** sheds some light on this phenomenon. **Chapter 10, Building a Bridge to the New You,** offers remedies in addition to the resources in the **Appendix**.

Others have asked, *"Is it possible to find your soulmate?"* To find our soulmates, we must know who we are looking for! These heart qualities of the Creator are our divine birthright contained within us. We must learn to align ourselves with our spirit to open the door to more happiness, peace, love, joy, and abundance. **Chapter 2**, **Relationship Karma**, and **Chapter 3**, **Relationship Vision**, guide us on what virtues to consider during our search.

The primal will of the divine is for the good of all. When I sit in silence with the Presence, I know all is well, and I can see and feel her presence moving closer to me with each breath. I sense a loving, powerful, sensual, wise, compassionate, beautiful, and abundant presence coming closer and closer with each breath. I feel this in my bones. As I align with my true self and she aligns with me, we become One. This healing of the masculine and feminine, first within oneself and then with another, is a spiritual journey of the highest order.

I offer these life lessons learned, blessings, realizations, strategies, and exercises that I have utilized over several decades that have propelled my personal and spiritual growth. There are self-reflection questions and tasks to complete to better understand my own dating experience and how I may need to evolve to find my soulmate.

Prologue

I am writing this book to help others on their journey to find their soulmate. The term "soulmate" means many things to different people. Here is my definition. My desire is for a life partner who has high character and knows how to love themselves, which enables them to share that love with others while living a healthy lifestyle. We complement each other and are compatible. They honor and respect themselves and our monogamous relationship. We genuinely support each other's dreams, goals, and relationship desires. Any dramas, traumas, or past relationships are over and left in the past. We have similar core values (e.g., honesty, transparency, integrity, etc.) that govern our lives. When challenges arise, as there will always be growth areas, they have the willingness, tools, and resources to deal with them and move forward.

Grit, willingness to grow and develop, transparency, and courage are critical qualities needed to change and transform. Learning more about myself gave me greater clarity about what is important, such as expressing my genuine desires, perceiving another person's "real" intentions, and choosing only healthy relationships in the future. Thus, my dating preferences evolved.

It has taken me several decades to figure this out. I have been married for over 25 years and divorced three times. I learned something from each relationship, which drove my personal and spiritual growth.

Initially, we seek experiences based on our role models (parents, relatives, and friends) and learn through trial and error. Our hopes are high when we first meet. As we spend time with someone, we experience them as they "really" are. Our past relationship Karma shapes our beliefs, behaviors, and actions. Karma is the total of our conscious and unconscious desires, beliefs, attitudes, drives, and actions accumulated over time. If we have experienced loving, supportive, honest, mentally and emotionally healthy, romantic, and monogamous relationships that lasted for over the years, then we set this as our karmic relationship baseline. Another key is being respectful of each other as individuals and our relationship.

As we become more experienced, some choose the path of "La Vida Loca." Their lives are filled with frequent partying, affairs, and old "friends" who they hook up with across years and even decades. However, the "high" they encounter is temporary, and they become trapped, continually seeking stimulus from outside of themselves to feel alive. If this is your life goal, enjoy it!

Yet, I have noticed that we seek more meaningful relationships as we age. We set goals of settling down when we hit 30. We date and seemingly only encounter "La Vida Loca" players. Then you hit 40! Next comes 50. Take a wild guess about what type of relationships they experience. Their past has become based on their unconscious choices. They are trapped because even though they say they want a good, stable relationship, they are "player players" who subconsciously choose other players and do not take responsibility for changing their mating choices. Where is their life partner who loves, supports, respects, and cares for them in a monogamous relationship?

Decades of living in "Tinder Land" do not prepare anyone for a loving, supportive, respectful, committed relationship. Romance novels and movies create a fantasy that things will just work out when you meet the right person. Decades of crazy, shallow, convenient sexual relationships do not build a foundation for a committed relationship, let alone marriage.

I wondered why most of the women I met who claimed they wanted to be in a monogamous long-term relationship did not know how to make that happen. Many thought it was okay to be a "side piece" even though their "friend" would never commit to them and treated them poorly. Yet, they desperately held on to them.

I am writing this book to share the lessons I have learned from my experience, research into human behavior, and spiritual psychology. The experiences in this book are not only my personal experiences. They are from stories that friends, fellow seekers, and family have shared with me. Let's begin our journey of "***From Profiles to Partners, A Successful Guide to Real Love: How to Attract, Recognize and Fall In Love with Your Soulmate.***

Chapter 1
Let the Games Begin

"Know Thy Self."–Plato

As I fill out my profile, I must describe myself. I know myself better than anyone else. However, this is not an autobiography. I am writing this as an introductory love note to my soulmate. Hmm?! How do I describe myself so that she recognizes me and responds from the dozens of profiles people skim through daily? How do I express my authentic self in an intriguing, fun, exciting way? What pictures do I select that highlight me? What kind of woman am I looking for? How am I going to sort through the responses?

To begin, I am a mature, handsome, active, tall, intelligent man in good health. I enjoy concerts, jazz, and walks on the beach. I enjoy science fiction, fantasy, mystery, romantic comedies, action movies, and books. My love languages are quality time, touch, and words of affirmation.

I know that "she" is out there somewhere. Perhaps in the virtual world of the dating apps, or I might run into her at Trader Joe's. How will I recognize her? How can I communicate that I am a loving, romantic, fun, intelligent, sensual, respectful, monogamous, spiritual, and successful man? How will I discern who she is from the dozens of people who pop up each day as I swipe left or right?

How will I figure out who are the diamonds in the rough deserving closer investigation versus the pretenders who have never been in loving, happy, fulfilling, exclusive, monogamous, honest, supportive, or respectful relationships?

I need some clarity to guide my decision-making. As I contemplate what I have learned over the years, I recognize how much I have evolved. What wisdom did I glean from these experiences? What part did I play in the game? Why did I not leave sooner? What must we do to make different, healthier relationship choices? What beliefs about myself must I let go of to move forward? How do I plot a different course for my future?

Exercises

    a. What type of man or woman am I?

    b. Does my profile provide only generic information or specific personal insights?

    c. What type of woman or man am I looking for?

d. What activities and interests would we share?

e. What are your deal breakers?

Chapter 2
Relationship Karma

"Three things cannot be long hidden: the sun, the moon, and the truth."–
Buddha

Why are some people lucky in love and others not? We all know people who met in high school, dated, graduated, and married. They have happy lives, are completely loyal to their wedding vows, and have loved and honored each other for decades. What secret do they possess? Are they lucky, or do they have good "Karma?"

The word "Karma" means "action." It means that our conscious and unconscious beliefs, behaviors, and habits, expressed as past actions, dictate our present and future. This is true until we "Wake Up" and transform our actions by reprogramming our beliefs, attitudes, and behaviors about ourselves, the opposite sex, and relationships. This evolution in consciousness can result in a more fulfilling and rewarding long-term relationship.

I have also encountered a second group of people. They may not marry but enjoy long-term loving, monogamous relationships that last for decades.

Next, we have people who sow their wild oats in their late teens or twenties and plan to marry when they turn 30. They go from party to party, affair to affair, year after year, and then decades. Then suddenly, they are in their 40s and 50s, desperately wondering where they went wrong. A brief moment of self-reflection leads many of them to the false conclusion that no "good" men/women are left. This, of course, is a false belief. Then how do we attract a compatible, loving, and stable person? What must we do differently?

This leads to another round of questions. First, does a life of wine, women/men, and song prepare us for a happy, loving, romantic, respectful, passionate, and stable relationship? What are the keys and heart qualities we must cultivate to prepare for a long-term, stable, loving, respectful, fulfilling, monogamous, supportive, and empowering relationship?

Here are some examples of heart qualities and behaviors from my list. Feel free to modify this with your own.

a. Honesty
b. Discernment
c. Clarity
d. High self-esteem
e. High self-respect and respect for others
f. Strong personal boundaries
g. Self-worthiness
h. Transparency
i. Integrity
j. Financially responsible: Do they know how to live on a budget?
k. Spiritually, mentally, and emotionally balanced
l. Compatibility and complementary with you
m. Lives a healthy lifestyle
n. Romantic
o. Has released past lovers: Are they emotionally available?
p. Willing to put the time into building a new relationship
q. Knows the difference between being lonely and alone
r. High moral code: no adultery, booty calls, orgies, or sex with minors
s. Do not numb themselves with parties, affairs, alcohol, or drugs
t. If they have a drama or trauma, they seek professional help to move their lives forward.

These virtues and heart qualities allow us to make self-empowering, loving, and honoring choices about our lives and relationships. These give us a powerful foundation to build relationships with people with similar values.

As you reflect upon each of these qualities, contemplate each relationship you have had, and think about how it played out, consider what different choices you can make about your actions and what to look for in your next relationship. Remember that the definition of insanity is repeating the same actions and expecting different results.

Transforming our Karma requires us to become spiritual warriors, step up to the plate, own our mistakes, and do the necessary work to clear the past unconscious way of living and build our spiritual muscles to make healthier, life-affirming choices. In the appendix, I am providing several references that I have drawn upon to assist me in my journey. These books, videos, and audio materials are written by internationally known leaders in their fields of psychology and personal and spiritual development. They are expert psychologists, therapists, and spiritual counselors who have helped thousands of people improve the quality of their lives.

Exercises

a. What heart qualities do you possess that make you an excellent life partner?

b. Why are these important to you?

c. What heart qualities should your partner possess?

d. Why are these important to you?

e. How have these qualities shown up in your past?

f. Which areas do you need to develop?

g. What must you release to create space for your soulmate?

Chapter 3
Relationship Vision: Why Do I Want a Relationship?

"Create a vision of who you want to be and how you want to live. Vision is a picture of the future that produces passion. Then act as if that picture is already true! "
–Arnold Schwartzenegger

Why Do I Want a Relationship?

What is your vision for how you want to live your relationship with your soulmate? What are your love languages? What activities do you want to share? Which activities do you want to share with friends? Where and how much do you want to travel? Where do you want to live? How much time do you want to spend together? How important is sex? How many times a week do you want to enjoy it? Do you live a healthy lifestyle? Do you enjoy hiking, or would you rather watch games on your days off? Do you want to go to concerts or watch Netflix on the weekend? Do you like to go out clubbing at night?

These are just some questions about yourself that you should reflect upon as you consider what you seek in a life partner. What habits, beliefs, and behaviors do you have, and what have you observed from your potential partners? I have come up with three categories as a starting point for your consideration:

1. Deal-breakers are nonnegotiable characteristics, behaviors, or habits that your significant other must absolutely embody. Here are some examples of deal-breakers:
   a. Honesty
   b. Attractiveness
   c. Lives a healthy lifestyle
   d. Romantic
   e. Transparent
   f. Drug-free
   g. Doesn't gamble
   h. Nonsmoker
   i. Love and accept themselves as they grow
   j. Knows how to accept love
   k. Has a regular self-care routine that they enjoy
   l. Knows how to share love
   m. Spiritually, mentally, and emotionally balanced
   n. Their word is their bond.
   o. Addiction-free
   p. Capable of having respectful disagreements
   q. Exes are in the past.
   r. Financially responsible
   s. Mutual caring, liking, and respect for each other
   t. Sexually compatible

2. Important are highly desired attributes, characteristics, or habits they should have. Here are some examples that may be important to you:
   a. Great sense of humor Enjoys sports
   b. Enjoys concerts
   c. Loves to hike
   d. Vegetarian

3. Nice-to-have qualities are very negotiable characteristics, behaviors, or habits that they might have. Here are some examples:
   a. Lives nearby
   b. Good cook

   c. Rams fan
   d. Warriors fan
   e. Cubs Fan
   f. Enjoys golfing
   g. Couch potato
   h. Runs 5ks and 10ks

4. What activities will you and your soulmate share?
   a. Vacations
   b. Bowling
   c. Hiking
   d. Dancing
   e. Weekend getaways
   f. Yoga retreats

<u>Exercises</u>

1. Review your list and analyze each quality and how you categorize it. I spent a couple of weeks revising my list as I thought about each relationship and what I learned about myself and the others. I revised my list at least ten times over several months.

2. Relationship Vision Meditation (Do this at least once a week.)
   a. Schedule time and find a quiet space to meditate.
   b. Sit in a comfortable chair with your back straight and feet on the ground.

c. Breathe deep, full-body breaths. Hold each one for a moment and exhale, completely emptying your lungs. Repeat this three times.

d. Continue your full-body breaths, relaxing, and say to yourself, "I am love," and deeply feel the love rising in you and vibrating around you for six breaths.

e. Now say, " I multiply this vibration of love by a factor of five. Continue this for six breaths.

f. Now say, " I multiply this vibration of love by a factor of ten. Continue this for six breaths.

g. Act as if you woke up in the morning together. What would you say to each other? What would you do together throughout the day?

h. Keep in mind the heart qualities you identified above. You are the director of this movie! Start from when you wake up. See, speak, and feel the scenes.

i. Relax and sit quietly for a few minutes at the end of the meditation.

j. After your last question, say, "I give thanks, and I know now that more is being revealed."

k. Open your eyes and sit quietly for a minute.

l. Enjoy this practice until your soulmate manifests.

Chapter 4
Dating Strategies: Seeing Beyond Appearances

"All that glitters is not gold."–William Shakespeare

Whether meeting someone in person or via a dating app, as amateur detectives, we call upon our intuition to guide our first impressions. What do their profiles tell us about the person and their temperament? Are they laid back, serious, or high-energy with a sense of humor? Ask yourself if this person were standing in front of you, what would you say to them? If I find them interesting, I think of something witty or funny to catch their attention. As I review their responses, I think about the effort they put into it. Does it reveal anything meaningful about them? Is it a thoughtful response or just an emoji?

When I find someone interesting, we begin texting back and forth. I discover she has many attractive qualities, is intelligent, and has a great personality. Then we may exchange numbers and talk. As I begin the call, I keep in mind using my wit and charm to see what they are really like. I keep the call to 30 minutes. This is plenty of time to size them up and see if you want to meet them in person.

Preparing for our first date, I establish criteria for what I want to learn. Take your top five items from **Chapter 3–Relationship Vision** and remember them for each date as something you want to know. When you have the next date, use the next five, and so on. (Be casual as you mix these questions with flirty small talk and read their body language.) Here are a few first-, second-, or third-date questions after you have established a rapport. Again, mix these questions in with playful banter. Be creative and come up with your own. Here are a few example questions for women to use:

1. Tell me about your lifestyle. What do you do to maintain or improve your overall health?
2. What was your best relationship, and why was it the best?
3. How long did your best relationship last?
4. How often did you see each other?
5. Why didn't it work? What aspects of the relationship didn't work for you? How was the communication between the two of you?
6. What did you learn about yourself through that relationship? What did you take away from that experience?
7. How long did your relationship last?
8. Did you have a stable home life? Which parent could you usually count on?
9. Are there any childhood memories that stand out as traumatic for you?
10. Parental relationship models: Were your parents happily married?
11. Have you had any affairs while in an exclusive relationship? What did you learn?
12. Why did you engage in the affair?
13. If you found out that your partner was cheating on you, how would you react?
14. I saw the craziest thing on Netflix: "90-Day Fiancé." By the way, have you ever experienced a polyamorous relationship?

<u>Additional Questions a woman might ask after meeting the person</u>

1. What do you envision a relationship at this stage would add to your life?
2. What areas of your life would you ideally like to invest in or share with your partner? Sharing your friends? Your Family?

Sharing a home? Sharing finances? Sharing in raising a child? Sharing a business?

3. How do you react when you feel hurt by an event or something someone said?
4. If I offended you, would you tell me?
5. What was your worst relationship and why? Note: Women are advised not to ask this question until we know the person or have had an in-person meeting.

Here are a few example questions for men to ask:

1. Do you live a healthy lifestyle?
2. What was your best relationship, and why was it the best?
3. How long did it last?
4. How often did you see each other?
5. What was your worst relationship and why?
6. Why didn't it work?
7. What did you learn about yourself?
8. How long did it last?
9. What was your childhood like? Did you have any childhood drama?
10. Parental relationship models: Were your parents happily married?
11. You have led an interesting life! Have you had any affairs?
12. Did you enjoy the affair? Why did you engage in the affair?
13. If you discovered someone cheated on you, what would you do?
14. I saw the craziest thing on Netflix: "90-Day Fiancé." By the way, have you ever experienced a polyamorous relationship?

<u>Additional Questions a man might ask after meeting the person</u>

1. I saw the craziest thing on Netflix. Have you ever been invited to an orgy?
2. I saw the craziest thing on Netflix. As a mature adult, have you ever had a sexual relationship with a minor?
3. I saw the craziest thing on Netflix. Have you had any bisexual experiences?

4. I saw this crazy show on Prime: " Married at First Sight." They discover crazy things about each other after they are married. By the way, how many partners have you had sex within the last 12 months?
5. How many partners have you had sex within the last 24 months?

Sum up what you have learned from the date. Do you want to go out with them on another date? Continue this process after each date and see where it takes you. If you are fortunate, you will meet someone you want to date repeatedly for several months. Our purpose is to share enough experience with a person to form an opinion on whether or not this is worth the investment of time, love, and money.

Exercises

a. Evaluate each of your dates based on your criteria.

____

____

____

b. How honest do you think they were?

____

____

____

c. When they asked you questions, did you respond honestly?

____

____

____

d. Do you want to move forward on a second date? If so, why?

Chapter 5
Let's Review Your Dating Experience

"The definition of insanity is doing the same thing over and over again and expecting different results."–Unknown (often attributed to Albert Einstein)

"You have to vibrationally become that which you seek to attract into your life."–Michael Beckwith

Most people only know each other at a surface level. Spending days and weekends together provides an excellent opportunity to see a person in many different situations. Being around each other, chilling and watching Netflix, or doing household chores provides fertile ground to understand how they live. What makes them happy and excited? How do they handle stress? Does the way they treat you change depending on their mood or who they are around? Are they a person with champagne tastes and beer money? Does the past relationship history they shared with you at the beginning still ring true? Do you respect and honor each other in public and private? Do you want to see if this relationship has legs, or do either of you consider it just a casual thing?

We must learn to trust our instincts when our intuition arises, and we feel something needs to be clarified. Regardless of how physically attractive, educated, cultured, busy, or successful they might be, that has little to do with a person's consciousness and character.

Ask yourself these questions:

1. Do you know the quality of any of their relationships in the last three years?
2. Are there any unknowns or discrepancies in their story?
3. Is this a long-term relationship or one that has promise? Why?
4. What evidence have you observed?
5. What is their attachment style? See the Appendix "The New Science of Adult Attachment" and take the free online quiz.

You should trust your intuition in the evaluation. Once again, these suggestions are only intended for those who genuinely desire a monogamous, long-term relationship.

How have you been living? The Law of Attraction states, "You attract what you are in consciousness." If you have poverty consciousness, you may have problems with money. If you have a victim's consciousness, you may attract abusive people. If you are a player, you will seek someone else's partner. If you are an adulterer, you will attract someone else's cheating spouse.

Relationships are not about finding a good woman or man. It is about becoming a man or woman of acute consciousness and character, preparing you for a loving, supportive, respectful, monogamous, stable, long-term relationship. What is your vision for the life you want to share with your soulmate?

The Life Visioning Process is an excellent reference for developing a vision of what you want to create. Two other excellent references are *No Matter What!: 9 Steps to Living the Life You Love* by Lisa Nichols and *We Do: Saying Yes to a Relationship with Depth, True Connection, and Enduring Love* by Dr. Stanley Tatkin. Each of these books is a bestseller and has helped people around the globe transform their lives.

Review Chapter 2, **Relationship Karma**, and think honestly about your past relationship challenges. If you have been a player and want to continue that lifestyle, you can put this book down now. If you are serious about doing the work and becoming a more stable, loving, and whole person, not addicted to the transitory seduction of wine, drugs, and sex, read on.

You should also quickly review **Chapter 6, Yellow Flags**, before the first date.

Exercises

a. Based on the heart qualities you consider essential to a successful relationship, how have you been living during:

____

____

____

- The last six months?

____

____

____

- The last year?

____

____

____

- The last three years?

b. If you are missing the mark based on your success criteria, what
    is the root cause?

c. What steps can you take to become the person you need to be to
    attract your soulmate?

d. How much time and effort are you willing to invest to live a
    more fulfilling and happier life for your own sake?

Chapter 6
Yellow Flags

"Fools rush in where Angels fear to tread."–Unknown

Here are some common yellow flags you may encounter. These are "proceed with caution" signs if you want a long-term, stable, monogamous, loving relationship and already live the "stable" core values discussed above. Several of these yellow flags can become red flags.

1) They spend a great deal of time grinding on their ex. It is normal to swap histories briefly and then flirt with each other. However, as the evening progresses, they keep returning to their ex and how they mistreated them. This person has lots of baggage and has not healed, nor do they want or know how to. They have been living this way for years, and they unconsciously seek the same dysfunctional relationship again and again. Ask them, "How can they develop a relationship with you while living in the past?"

2) They have long-term sexual relationships with multiple people spanning years who will never marry them. They do not know how to choose a loving, stable relationship.

They date people who bluntly tell them they will never marry them. The desperate, lonely person stays in the relationship, hoping this attitude will change. After years of pouring themselves into the relationship, they tell the player they want more commitment. Of course, they say no. The unsatisfying relationship ends, and they look again and find the same type of "player," and the cycle starts again.

3) When you first meet, you swap histories and move into creating your relationship. Then suddenly, out of the clear blue sky, they start talking about all the great times with their "ex" lovers.

4) They tell you what they think you want to hear and have no opinions of their own.

5) They say their psychic told them that you were their soulmate! You should recognize this special connection based on your inner guidance and interactions with them over time. You do not need an external agency to declare this.

6) They claim to desire a long-term relationship that could lead to marriage, even though they have never enjoyed a stable, committed, loving relationship. They planned to sow their wild seeds until age 30 and then marry. Thirty became 40 and then 50, etc. They are alone, desperate, and caught in Tinder land, floating from person to person, settling for affairs. They are stuck until they hit rock bottom. This is an ideal time for them to seek professional help, enabling them to turn their life around.

7) At the beginning of the relationship, you both call, text each and spend time together regularly. Over time, only one person is putting forth the effort. You ask them about what is going on. Their answer is vague. Your prospective partner has become distracted by someone or something else.

Exercises

a. How many yellow flags have you encountered in the last:

- Three months?

- Six months?

- One year?

---

b. How many yellow flags have you personally flown in the last six months?

---

c. What actions can you take to remedy these growth areas?

Chapter 7
Red Flags

"Danger, Will Robinson!"–Lost In Space
"I pity the fool."–Mr. T

Here are some common red flags you may encounter. These are "stop signs" if you want a long-term, stable, monogamous relationship and are already living the "stable" core values discussed in Chapter 2.

1) The Disappearing Act: They claim they are not in a relationship. However, they are not available consistently to spend days with you. Or they only text and want to come by late at night.

2) They keep mementos of their conquests and brag about them. When you ask about their relationship, they claim they are just friends, and it was a long time ago. However, their body language and voice convey that there is much more to the story! Ask them when the last time they saw them. How often do they see each other? When was the last time they slept together? This will lead to a fascinating discussion. Keep in mind that you are always teaching people how to treat you. If your intuition says something is off, pay attention.

3) Has the person never been married or had a long-term loving, respectful, and supportive monogamous relationship? Perhaps they dedicated themselves to their career and lived a life of wine, men/women, and song.

They are living "La Vida Loca" and see the opposite sex as objects. As they age, they claim to be more seasoned and now know how to settle down. However, as you spend time with them, it becomes clear they maintain sexual and emotional relationships with many of their so-called "exes" over the years. More disturbingly, they continue to hook up whenever it is convenient for them. These are long-term, hook-up relationships. It will be difficult, if not impossible, for them ever to have a monogamous relationship with a stable, loving person.

These karmic tendencies undermine their ability and capacity to love themselves or anyone else meaningfully. They are addicted to the adrenaline rush of being the side piece, and even though they wish for more, they cannot change these decades-long habits. They will attempt to deceive you about these relationships and call them "friends."

4) Your partner flirts with another person when you are out on a date. Clearly, they have no respect for your relationship, themselves, or you.

5) No one tells you everything at once. Over time, their stories change. At first, they were the loyal spouse or partners who stood by their relationship(s). Over time, they reveal they are polyamorous, enjoy adultery, etc. When you ask them about the details, they claim they now had an "open" relationship and their partner was also cheating. Once again, their true nature is revealed.

6) Out of the clear blue sky, they reveal they enjoyed the affairs because they were the "fantasy escape" for the adulterer from the burden of the spouses and children. A common excuse is they cheated on their partners because they could not satisfy them sexually, and they needed a release. Or they claim they had an "open relationship." Of course, their partner didn't know about this "open relationship."

7) They put minimal effort into spending quality time with you because they are tired. However, when a friend calls to go out, suddenly they are energized, in the shower, getting their sexy on, and out the door!

9) They receive texts and calls from friends of the opposite sex early in the morning and late at night.

They continue to nurture their so-called "past" relationships that were not good for them via texts, calls, and social media.

10) They want to keep their dating profiles active after your relationship becomes exclusive.

<u>Exercises</u>

   a. How many red flags have you encountered in the last:

 • Three months?

 • Six months?

 • Year?

   b. How many red flags have you personally flown in the last:

 • Three months?

 • Six months?

 • Year?

   c. What actions can you take to remedy these growth areas?

These yellow and red flags are just examples of dysfunctional behaviors to be wary of. People are not like fine wine; they do not get better with time.

The appendix has several self-help books and videos from professional therapists and healers. They are experts who assist unconscious people in transforming themselves as they confront and release their dysfunctional behaviors and learn new life-affirming beliefs about themselves, life, and the opposite sex, thus transforming their lives to enjoy stable, loving, respectful, passionate relationships.

Chapter 8
What If I Keep Repeating the Same Dating Experiences?

"It's like déjà vu all over again."–Yogi Berra

"The struggles along the way are only meant to shape you for your purpose."
–Chadwick Boseman

"How can I expand in a world that seems to be shrinking? How can I evolve when everything seems to dissolve right in front of me? How can I become more of myself when the world seems to be crumbling right in front of me? How can I have more prosperity? *Something within me knows that the answer is within me all the time. I can think independent of the problem or situation because of a faculty given me by the universal presence. This means I can enter into a co-creation with the universal presence which will change my life."*
–*The Answer is You* by Michael Beckwith

If you consistently have the same dating experiences, this demonstrates the universal law of Karma in action! Change requires expanded consciousness and a transformation of our beliefs, attitudes, habits, and behaviors. How important is it to you to enjoy a loving, supportive, romantic, respectful, abundant, empowering relationship? We must create a sacred space within ourselves while being patient and available to welcome our soulmate into our lives.

The effort to change, grow, and evolve requires commitment, focus, courage, and unflinching honesty about how we have lived for years and perhaps several decades. Our unconscious mental and emotional drives, habits, attitudes, and behaviors can show up as procrastination and resistance to personal growth, resulting in the same dating and life experiences. Your subconscious has been programmed to accept dysfunctional behaviors as your norm, and it takes effort to pull the weeds out of your subconscious garden to create room for the new life you want to create. Here are some remedy options.

A. Reread the following chapters with open-mindedness and courage to separate your egoic self from your actual behavior.

1. Watch the "Watch the Answer is You" video link in the appendix. It is a powerful source of inspiration when we seem "stuck." As you perform the exercises in the video, your mind will open to new possibilities.

2. **Reread Chapter 2–Relationship Karma:** Start fresh, be honest about your behavior and dating choices, and complete the exercises anew.

3. **Reread Chapter 3–Relationship Vision:** Start fresh, be honest about your behavior and dating choices, and complete the exercises anew.

4. **Reread Chapter 4–Dating Strategies:** Start fresh, be honest about your behavior and dating choices, and complete the exercises anew. What differences do you notice between the first time you went through the exercises and now? You should see significant differences in your choices.

5. **Reread Chapters 5 and 6–Red and Yellow Flags:** What yellow and red flags have you observed with your dates, and when did you see them? Did you ask them questions for clarity? If you stayed, why? If you left, how long did it take you and why? Do you have clarity on your personal growth areas now?

6. Use the practices from **Chapter 10–Building the Bridge to the New You**.

B. Pick one or more books from the Appendix, study them, and practice the exercises.

C. Go to my website and book a session.

www.fromprofilestopartners.love and schedule a Dating Coaching session.

Chapter 9
The Road to a Long-Term Relationship

"Everywhere I'm lookin' now, I'm surrounded by your embrace. Baby, I can see your halo."–Beyonce

Based upon what you have experienced over the months and perhaps years, ask yourself if this person is someone who has the life experience necessary to cultivate a monogamous long-term relationship that could lead to marriage or not. Take the time to evaluate their stories and your experience with them.

Here are several evaluation criteria to use as a lens. What is your perception of them in each of these categories? What importance do you attach to these? If you have other qualities you feel are essential, add them. If you are just looking for a good time, ignore them. Be honest about what kind of person you are and what you seek.

a. **Honesty:** Only you know who you really are. What is your heart's desire? What are you doing to grow and improve yourself and your life circumstances? What are your and their growth areas? Do any of these yellow or red flags apply to you?

b. **Discernment:** Life is a mirror. What you have experienced so far in your relationships mirrors your subconscious programming. We must take ownership of our past decisions and mistakes to grow. You may have played games along the way. Now is the moment to make different empowering choices and create a new life. The definition of insanity is to make the same choices and expect different results. What tools and techniques are available to you to grow?

c. **Clarity:** The law of attraction demonstrates that to have something, you must become it in consciousness. All of your thoughts, words, and deeds must be in alignment. Do you genuinely desire a loving, supportive, passionate, romantic, joyful, monogamous relationship? How have you been living? In what areas do you come up short? What subconscious blocks are there?

d. **Worthiness:** Do you believe you are worthy of a loving, supportive, passionate, romantic, joyful, monogamous relationship? What are the obstacles that have kept you from achieving this already? Are there any subconscious blocks from your past? How will you clear these?

e. **Transparency:** Our actions should be consistent with our thoughts, words, and deeds. If unexpected challenges arise, we deal with them openly and honestly. We communicate with our prospective partners this way and expect nothing less from them.

f. **Integrity:** Your thoughts, words, and deeds are in alignment. When you are in a committed relationship, act accordingly. Players will always test you to see if you are just a poser. Are you one of those in the club looking for action in the evening and in church on Sunday singing "Praise the Lord?"

If someone asks you out while you are in a relationship, do you tell them you cannot meet them for a drink, dinner, or coffee? It is not a player's responsibility to respect your relationship. It is yours alone. Your actions define you. If you want to align with the values of a committed relationship, you must start living that way now!

How have the years and decades served you in cultivating a loving, supporting, empowering romantic relationship with your old dating patterns and your circle of "friends?" Your choices define you. Be honest with yourself. If you want to continue being a player in "Tinder Land," keep repeating the same patterns and watch the decades fly by. You may unconsciously believe that "there are no good men/women around." Of course, this is not true. Your subconscious is attuned to living in "Tinder Land," and you do not know how to live otherwise. You are comfortable with your discomfort.

g. **<u>Financially responsible</u>:** Do they live within their means? Or do they have champagne taste and beer money?

h. **<u>Spiritual, mental, and emotional balance</u>:** We have our own personal relationship with the divine. We honor this relationship via meditation, prayer, expressing our genuine intentions, and high-consciousness actions as we live and engage with others.

i. **<u>Compatibility and complementary</u>:** Do you genuinely enjoy and like each other? When there is no party, alcohol, etc., and it's just the two of you, do you enjoy each other's company?

j. **<u>Respectful</u>:** Are you respectful about how you treat your partner, and are they respectful to you? A simple way to think about this is to work backward from the end goal. How a husband and wife treat each other should embody love, romance, respect, support, monogamy, etc. Are the qualities of a fiancé/fiancée any different? How about your monogamous relationship? I contend that if they are not demonstrating these qualities once you agree to it, they will not change once they have a ring on their finger. Use your intuition to discern how you and your partner behave. Accept no excuses or rationalization for bad behavior. Our lives, time, and energy have great value. Deal with situations when they come up and ask real questions.

k. **Romantic:** What are your and your partner's languages of love? Discuss what you consider romantic and ask what your partner enjoys as you engage.

l. **Available:** Are you available to each other? Or do they have a party to go to with their friends? Review the yellow and red flags section!!!

m. **Monogamy:** This is a mutually exclusive relationship. You must release the lesser to receive the greater to create space for new love to grow. Let go of your current and past lovers to allow a new relationship to evolve. It's a fundamental betrayal of trust when playing the game of "we are just friends."

I am often asked what is the difference between a long-term exclusive relationship and a marriage. If both people are open to marriage and you meet all the criteria for a successful relationship, why not? Some people want monogamy just because of their past. I believe that relationships should evolve as we do. Their joint vision can propel them forward as a foundation of love, trust, respect, support, and the healing of wounds progress.

n. **Self Love:** It is a commitment to our personal happiness and well-being through self-compassion, acceptance, and kindness. We must balance self-kindness, self-acceptance, self-nurturing, self-support, self-restraint, self-responsibility, and self-persistence. These focus areas play out in our relationships with 1) ourselves, 2) our family, 3) dating and mating, and 4) society.

Signs of self-love can include:

a. Setting and upholding personal boundaries.
b. Using positive self-talk and not harsh criticism.

   c. Being kind and forgiving to yourself if you make a mistake or
      feel inadequate.
   d. Treating yourself with empathy as you would a friend
      experiencing the same challenge.
   e. Taking part in activities that promote your mental and physical
      well-being.
   f. Valuing yourself enough to pursue new goals or learn new skills.
   g. Accepting your strengths and weaknesses to let go of
      unreasonable expectations.
   h. Considering yourself rather than always putting others first.
   i. Celebrating or acknowledging your achievements.
   j. Feeling comfortable living by your personal beliefs and
      values rather than conforming to external standards.

Exercises

   a. Build a list of qualities that are important to you.

   b. Ask yourself why these are important.

   c. Ask yourself how many of these values you are living.

   d. Why do you think you have not yet met a partner with these
      virtues?

   e. Update **your Chapter 3—Relationship Vision** meditation
      based on your discoveries!

Chapter 10
Building a Bridge to the New You!
Transformational Tools and Techniques

"The secrets of alchemy exist to transform mortals from a state of suffering and ignorance to a state of enlightenment and bliss."–Deepak Chopra

"We are vibrational beings. When we lift our vibration to what we want to experience, it happens first on a vibratory level, and it shows up and manifests in our life. So people who are holding onto deceit, unforgiveness, self-denial, victim consciousness, rancor, animosity, etc., are slowing down their vibration. Another way of saying it is <u>you cannot have what you are not willing to become vibrationally</u>."–Michael Beckwith

"Holding onto anger is like drinking poison and expecting the other person to die."–Buddha

We have the power within us to change our lives. The Presence within us is waiting to be recognized and summoned to support and co-create significant shifts in our lives. These transformational tools and techniques are well-known to therapists, counselors, and mystics.

We have done quite a lot of soul-searching and discovery on this journey of self-discovery!

Let's recap what we have accomplished so far. We have:

1. Built an authentic profile.

2. Examined our past relationship Karma and developed a life-affirming list of heart qualities as evaluation criteria for our search.
3. Developed a strategy and criteria to select prospective mate(s).
4. Performed a sanity check. What have I learned about them and myself? How do I become a better person and make better choices about who I invest my time, love, and energy with?
5. Learned to check for yellow flags that show some typical "proceed with caution" signs of an immature person.
6. Learned to check for red flags that show some "immediate stop" signs of an unstable person.
7. Employed success keys to evaluate whether the relationship is a candidate for a successful LTR based on your personal virtues and heart qualities list.
8. Developed your soulmate template to work with in meditation.
9. Developed strategies for moving forward if we keep repeating the same dating experiences.

We must have a strong personal conviction about becoming our authentic selves. Many people have been hypnotized into believing that when the right person comes along, they will instantly transform into a monogamous, honest, loyal, transparent, loving, and supportive spouse. This is a myth. Over 50 % of marriages end in divorce because of unresolved karmic issues. Second marriages have an even higher failure rate. We must embrace our immaturities with great conviction and deep compassion toward ourselves as we make the changes that will enhance our self-love, worth, esteem, and care for our own benefits and prepare us to share these heart qualities with another mature person.

We all have immaturities we must work on developing in different areas.

This chapter and the resource section provide tools and techniques for personal and spiritual development.

1. **Affirmations:** Affirmations are a powerful tool for spiritual growth and development. They can assist us in unwinding many of the subconscious beliefs we're programmed with by society, family, media, and other sources. The subconscious

mind is like a child. It accepts anything you unconsciously accept seven times or more as a personal law until you reprogram it. It takes 28 consecutive days for a new belief or habit to be solidified.

Two of the most powerful words we can speak are "I AM ..." I am powerful. I am worthy of love. I have abundance and prosperity. I am love, etc. It is a great practice to use these "I Am" affirmations each day for 28 days as you stand in front of a mirror, look yourself in the eyes, and proclaim them powerfully. Write down any qualities you want to cultivate and spend time each day affirming the truth of your being. After you have finished with the affirmations, sit in silence for five minutes, which anchors this new consciousness. Here are some of my favorites:

1.1 I AM Affirmations

I am the soul,
I am the light divine.
I am love,
I am will,
I am the perfect design.

I am, I am,
I am the Christ mind,
I am, I am.

I am allowing the Christ mind to think Truth through me,
I am. I am.
I am allowing the Christ mind to express Truth through me,
I am, I am.

1.2 Soulmate Call

Sit comfortably with your spine straight, chin forward, and quietly in a space where you will not be disturbed.
Close your eyes and take slow, even full-body breaths for several minutes, releasing everything.

Now, visualize a brilliant, luminous pink flame blazing in your heart center. This is the flame of divine love—the most powerful, magical, creative, transformative flame of the divine.

Breathe this pink flame into your heart center and feel its loving power. With each breath, feel it grow brighter and brighter.

Now, expand it throughout your abdomen. Next, extend your head and legs. Expand it further, six feet in all six directions. Feel the love. Feel it and visualize yourself radiating and receiving love from all directions. Breathe the love in and out.

Now, visualize your soulmate. See and feel them walking toward you. You smile at each other and talk. Visualize spending time together. Breathe life into this dream. Now, take one last deep breath and pour your love into your soulmate. See them enveloped in this cloud of love. Take another breath and hold it and then send it to your love.

Now relax and say, "So be. So it is. It is done."

2. **Meditation:** Meditation is a powerful tool for communing with your true self and your "I AM" Presence. There are many names for the Presence of God, including God, Source, Jesus Christ, Holy Spirit, IHVH, Krishna, Soul, Higher Self, Buddha, Allah, Great Spirit, etc., depending upon your culture and upbringing.

Sitting in silence allows the connection to strengthen. You will find peace, love, truth, and much more as you enjoy this. To begin, set a timer for five minutes and become aware of your breath. Take slow, long, full-body breaths for a count of four, then breathe out for a count of four. Focus on your heart as you breathe in and out. If any thoughts arise, allow them to drift by like a leaf blowing in the wind. Do not chase the thoughts that may come up. Stay calm, relaxed, and focused on your breath and heart as you enjoy this communion. As you get comfortable with this basic practice, extend the time from five minutes to 15, then from 15 to 30 minutes.

3. **Counseling:** Counseling is a powerful tool for "transformation." We are like players in the game of life. As we live our lives, we often cannot see how we are sabotaging ourselves. We need a coach to help us take our lives to the next level. Reading books is a good start. However, consistently putting these transformational changes into practice and being held accountable for results is another matter. I have worked with many practitioners and spiritual teachers for years. Each has provided vital insights that would have taken me many years to uncover on my own. These valuable insights assisted me in transmuting my lead to gold as I became the spiritual warrior I am. I have included several reference books and links to videos from leading therapists and counselors for your consideration.

4. **Release and Forgiveness**

   We must create space within ourselves by releasing the dramas and traumas of our past so new love can grow. Forgiving others and ourselves for our immaturity creates that space to move forward with our lives. We must forgive "them" for their actions. We must forgive ourselves for choosing to participate with them. Lisa Nichols, who wrote *"No Matter What!: 9 Steps to Living the Life You Love,"* has some excellent exercises for releasing and forgive*ness.

Another key to attracting and bonding with your soulmate is *open-mind-edness.* As we build the vision of our heart's desire for our soulmate and the life we will share, we must look for intuitive signs to guide us to the right person. This book offers a blueprint that can assist you. However, real guidance comes from our hearts and minds, always present with us and willingly guiding us as we learn to listen and trust its guidance. Based upon our relationship vision, a world of new possibilities opens for us to move forward, holding space for our soulmate to manifest.

Working with Transformational Therapists, Spiritual Practitioners, and Energy Healers can accelerate your healing journey.

As Albert Einstein famously said, "We cannot solve our problems with the same level of thinking that created them." My spiritual journey has brought me into contact with many master teachers of the Ageless Wisdom. I have learned many alternative techniques for healing wounds, trauma, and drama. The tools and techniques can also remove the false and limiting beliefs from the subconscious mind we are programmed with by historians, media, and other societal gatekeepers.

Use the link to my website below to schedule a session.

I hope you find the information here helpful. I wish you the best in your pursuit *From Profiles to Partners–A Successful Guide to Real Love: How to Attract, Recognize, and Fall In Love with Your Soulmate.*

Appendix

Amir Levine, M.D. and Rachel S.F. Heller, M.A., *The New Science of Adult Attachment and How It Can Help You Find—and Keep—Love* https://a.co/d/641Iw8O.

Stanley Tatkin, PsyD MFT, *We Do: Saying Yes to a Relationship of Depth, True Connection, and Enduring Love* https://a.co/d/gNZydIc.

Lisa Nichols, *No Matter What!: 9 Steps to Living the Life You Love* by https://a.co/d/hoZYKkv.

"Vow Village Interviews with Happily Married Couples" https://www.youtube.com/watch?v=s4FW7qs5PdE.

Michael Beckwith, *Life Visioning: A Transformative Process for Activating Your Unique Gifts and Highest Potential* My Book.

Dr. David R. Hawkins, M.D., Ph.D., *The Map of Consciousness Explained*. Veritas Publishing.

Edward J. Jones's website offers Dating Coaching advice and Energy Healing services to help you clear subconscious energy blocks, and downloads assist you in making your transition to a new "You" easier. www.fromprofilestopartners.love

Aylaiynah Garibay's *Centre for One Consciousness Leadership* provides insight into our soul's purpose utilizing the 22 mystical tokens of ageless wisdom. https://www.centreforoneconsciousleadership.net/

Ester Nicholson has created a wonderful, compassionate healing modality. Her Soul Recovery therapy has helped people around the globe. https://www.esternicholson.com/

Michael Beckwith, *The Answer is You*, https://www.youtube.com/watch?v=UEkE77itolM.

Hope Gillette, "Practicing Self-Love to Improve Well-Being." https://psychcentral.com/health/what-is-self-love-and-why-is-it-so-important.